FACES AND FRAMES

TALIA ANN GREEN

Copyright © 2020 by Talia Ann Green

All Rights Reserved. No part of this book may be performed, recorded, used or reproduced in any manner whatsoever without the written consent of the author and the permission of the publisher except in the case of brief quotations embodied in critical articles and review.

An imprint of Assure Press Publishing & Consulting, LLC

www.assurepress.org

Publisher's Note: Assure Press books may be purchased for educational, business, or sales promotional use. For information please visit the website.

Faces and Frames/ Talia Ann Green — 1st ed.

Cover art by Anthony Wilson

ISBN-13: 978-1-7335897-8-9
Library of Congress Control Number: 2020943798
eISBN-13: 978-1-7335897-9-6

CONTENTS

I

An Ode to Instability	3
My Mother's Garden	4
A Window in September	5
A Moment in Solitude, 1	6
Westwood	7
Sleep Paralysis	8

II

On Anorexia	11
The House on Blue Hill Street	12
Melting Snow	14
Morning Meditation	15
On Darker Days	16
The Siddur in Our Kitchen	17

III

On Faces and Frames	21
On a Painting (Cape Cod Morning — Hopper, 1950)	22
A Moment in Solitude, 2	23
On the Armless Statue on my Living Room Counter	24
The Spoon in my Cereal Bowl	25
On a Poem	26

IV

On Recovery	29
On a Good Day	31
A Walk after Dinner	32
Porcelain Woman	33
Late Blooming	34

About the Author 35

FACES AND FRAMES

I

An Ode to Instability

Here's to unstable grounds—
When the soil slopes sideways,
sudden shifts, tectonic
shock from still terrain—
Your toes dig for traction
but this shaky Earth is indifferent
to your desire for balance.

Here's to this shaky Earth—
To quivers from its core,

to   quakes   that   unsteady   your   kneecaps,
to ruptures that scare your spine straight.

Shockwaves send bristles up your back,
raise hairs across your arms.
    You imprint the Earth's sideways into your normal.

Here's to caves and crevasses,
potholes and mudslides.
Here's to facing unforeseen slopes,
to scaling the motion
when it is unchangeable.

Stillness is in the valley
between eruptions.
Let the grounds condition your feet
to surf wind gusts up
and glide back down, when the air slows.

My Mother's Garden

Gather me in bundles
of my backyard garden—
my red radish elbows,
my honey crisp palms,

the lavender budding along my jawline,

chardonnay grape vines
in wreaths around my wrists—
Thorns prick my knuckles,

but care for them.

Rake me clean of the bindweeds
germinating behind my ears.
Harvest the black cherries
pitted down my arms.

Tuck them under my shoulder blade,
and cherish the sweet seedlings
you'll see sprouting, in time.

A Window in September

Yellow carpet foliage.
Amber leaves matted with rainfall,
pressed by stepping sneaker soles
and ironed by baby carriage wheels.

Ruffles lift with the wind,
catch breeze under loose edges,

but these leaves hold their ground.
Steadfast, stubborn like concrete.
Mark their sidewalk space
and weave Autumn rugs
from curb to doorframe.

Here, a blanket to catch our footfalls.
Threads pile to cushion our heels,
cradle the weight of our hurry
as we grind our boots into its impermanence
—Its life is a temporary thing.

A welcome mat for cooler days.
These leaves invite us
until winter crawls too close
to appeal to our strolling.

A Moment in Solitude, 1

Peanut butter loneliness
spreads generous over my gums.

I keep my jaws shut
and roll my tongue around the gooey solitude
oozing between my teeth—
A snack for a silent mouth.

Westwood

A town, turning.
Corners of recycled streets
frame shiny cars
queued before red lights,
and a bank teller salivates
for a Friday-night feast,
and another door is boarded and marked:

For Rent.
Local windows watch, hollowed.
Make room for more elite.

What of these worn buildings?

A convenience store, gifted from father to son.
A shoemaker's counter-top, dusted.
He lived upstairs, once.

Windows see and have seen,
polished and purified.
Scrubbed of fingerprints
that pressed from the inside.
A generation's farewell.

Visitors peer in, anxious and waiting.
What will fill these furbished floors,
rebirthing behind oiled doors?

Sleep Paralysis

Last night I dreamt
we were hosting a dinner—
both of our hands caked
with uncooked food
and thinning time—
I baked bread
as the kitchen clock
jabbered like an in-law,
and when I reached for the cinnamon,
the bottle slipped from my hands
and fragmented on the floor.

And when I looked up to you,
you were unfamiliar.
So sure, I was, I followed the recipe
but your skin was singed—
your perfume curdled,
soured the inside of my nose.

Today,
when I reached across the sink
to brush my teeth,
my elbow hit the porcelain bowl
that held your makeup.
It fell to the floor, fragmented—
your blush like dried blood
against the ceramic tile.

II

On Anorexia

You remain
lodged in my teeth.
Too cozy in that crease
between tongue and cheek,
and your foul taste plasters my gums
in sticky quarantine.

Your morning breath gags me,
your fumes singe my lips,
gurgle back toward my lungs—
I inhale you, so off-putting.
You consume me in dinner leftovers.

I try to scrape you
with my pinky nail,
floss you from my wholeness,
and still, you suck your tummy in tight
and hide between toothbrush bristles—

> *a naughty child crouches in corn*
> *stalks, scraped knees,*
> *ignoring the third dinner*
> *call as the sky grows dim*
> *and the porch light flickers.*

The House on Blue Hill Street

Like clouds,
I build people from windowsills—
fill in sketchpads of their panes
with Monday nights.
Prints of tennis tournaments
suspend from fridge magnets,
notes for phyllo dough
fray thumbtacked to a cork overhang—
the recipe, a family heirloom;
the cork, left behind by the home's
previous owners.

Faces eclipse
across channels of glass.
I step,
study a perspective painting—

Feather lines
fringe a single mother's eyes
because *Jeopardy* skips
on her ex-husband's TV box—
faulty cable from a man of faults—
and unpopped kernels fumble
between her buttered fingers,
lodge between stitches
of a faux Persian,
also from a past love.

Upstairs, a page
from a child's coloring book.
A baby wriggles in a bassinet
between dreams
of her mother's heartbeat
and a father's Sunday humming,
too young to draw lines
between memory and imagining.

A house of drawings
strung up by cedar boards
on Blue Hill Street—
existence in outlines,
like an artist's sketchbook
flipped open by the wind.

Melting Snow

When pearl becomes invisible,
its glisten reduced to translucence
and alabaster drips
through the porch cracks.
It dims the wooden boards
during its downfall.

Does it bring with it splinters?
Does it soak its route and gather trinkets,
chilled remembrances
of grounds on which it stood?

Ice patches downsize in the morning.
Silver layers strip, its droplets
hung beneath the shade
of the porch's under-boards.

An iteration of itself.
Sharp in its being,
a jagged snapshot
of winter, for now.

Morning Meditation

Morning, mind yourself. Stay.
Leave your fingerprints as you pass by.
Mug pressed, rim indents my cheek.

Steam uplifts,
caffeinates my forward gaze—
Rouse my vision past noontime.

Your presence is a slipped penny.
Face obscured, peripheral luck.
I let you sit, shaded.

Afternoon will expose you
when its schedule strikes time.

On Darker Days

Then who watches us
in the overcast moments?

When bad days eclipse,
spread in clumps like frozen butter,
rolling with it grains of stale bread
and we curl, quaking from its chill?

Then who praises us
when the work is done?

Our achievements
like almond flour across our palms,
residue from the perfect batch, eaten—
We leave our hands unwashed.

I watch yesterday
from my bedside window,
licking his fingers clean,
and I listen to today's tummy grumbling
against the hum of my ceiling fan.

The Siddur in Our Kitchen

My *Saba's* prayer book
idles on a pedestal
of magazines and opened mail,
receipts and peanut crumbs,
its borders, embroidered,
a mantlepiece for yesterday things.

It reclines against routine,
drapes a holy face
over our coupon clippings—

And I see my *Saba* in its binds.
Hear his humming
swell from the pages,
pressed closed.
His scar, a crease in the spine.
His smile glints in the cross-stitching.

And he soaks his perch with his prayers,
my grandfather on our kitchen table.

III

On Faces and Frames

His nose blurs
from this side of the pane.

Fingertips smudge his fine lines,
swipe his detail sideways,
sweep across an oval, beige.
It's a dirty window I watch behind.

On seeing an outline—
an unconceived sketch.
Nameless by distance
and palm prints
by steps, uncounted,
from car door to coffee shop.
This pane, a film.

I fill his face with my stories.
A name under his tired eyes,
a wife across his bottom lip,
career in his jawline—
His blur is a wanting canvas.

Framed, made real.
This pane, a gallery.
His blur eclipses behind a car door, closing.
Stories rev with his engine.

Leave me to witness a street side exhibit, anonymous things.

On a Painting (Cape Cod Morning — Hopper, 1950)

From this angle, it appears
a landscape breathes on static glass,
oils rouged with expertise
careen to match the swaying grass—
branches taunt my unscathed knees,
pregnant clouds extol my tears—

and I have sat and watched for years.
Confined inside a cultured class
to study pastel willow trees
and watch the world slowly, slowly pass—
perhaps when no one's left to please
I'll wander where the painting clears

A Moment in Solitude, 2

A recluse. I watch
subject to my post—
over there, across the way. I watch
an untouchable world. I marvel
at closed circles,
comfortable silences,
her eyes cast down at her book,
his lost in daydreams. I wonder

how they can be in solitude
with their elbows grazing so gingerly,
as they are.

On the Armless Statue on my Living Room Counter

She leans,
hip juts in clay skirts,
a cloth cast, wrapped.
Glazed domestication.

Her waist pinched in naked air,
goosebumps smoothed
by artist hands and oven heat.
Hair pleated. Braided permanence.

And her eyes cast down,
and she always remembers what she's missing.

Phantom elbows bend,
shadow fingers mingle at the torso.
Raise lilies for her motion, in memory.

Her reminiscing, an apparition.
Her imaginings, a coy thing.
Envision what was,
her fantasies. Haunt her.

Stone dreams
of fingers twitching, arthritic pain,
palms pricked by lily stems
and sharp leaves, gripping.

The Spoon in my Cereal Bowl

It's one among many. Delicate curve,
ballerina limb elongates bowl-side—
silver extension, perfect steel stillness.

Marvel at its patience; its waiting; its breath.
Centered, glisten under kitchen lights—
statured posture precedes its practiced steps.
Envious limbs of similar skill stare,

sidelined. Pointed toes peak behind curtains,
half-drawn drawers, veteran steppers. They watch—
glimmering faces accumulate dust;
arches grow stiff in backstage clusters.

My spoon inhales stardom, readies its steps.
Brief eight-count breaths before its closing stretch,
sidelined again—too, one among many.

On a Poem

If I can't find love,
I matchmake my poems.
Words coalesce and test their phrases,
taste pronunciation,
bite their tongue on slant rhymes—
their sounds just slyly, coyly align.

Note their mingling, my words—curious, ambiguous.

Their verse tentative
until written declarative,
shy until printed
and bound.

And still,
my line breaks threaten longevity,
my page tears corrupt
a poem's cohesion,
my fragile art.

Thrive in your early drafts.
Find meaning in your deletion
if you don't make it past

this rough couplet
this rushed conclusion.

IV

On Recovery

הכל יהיה בסדר.[1]

My mother gifted me
her mantra, her syrup reprise—
Saccharine coats my fatigue,
my thoughts and slow steps,
candied by her mantra.

הכל יהיה בסדר.

My heels soak its words,
toes submerge
between its honeyed spaces.
Knees, immobile—
I am forced to breathe,
and I breathe its sweetness.

הכל יהיה בסדר.

"Lean into corners," *Ima* tells me,
"and cushion their peppered crevices with syrup."

"Taste the sharpness
bitter at the base of your throat,
but taste first the syrup,
my mantra's sweetness."

הכל יהיה בסדר.

1. Hebrew for *Everything will be okay.*

On a Good Day

On mornings like this,
the unkempt edges of my perspective
are tailored with gilded lace,
stitched in such a way
that I can't look at it straight
but its iridescence
reflects into my vision
and I watch the world
with gold in my eyes.

A Walk after Dinner

An hour of silhouettes:
Leaves like sponged paint pressed
against clean linen—
branches brushed with ebony
in a heavy hand,
and dusted with amber streetlight—
trunks like wet pastels,
soaking into sleeping mulch.

This hour is its own shadow,
itself and its outline.

A tree's roots lengthen
behind the drying oils
of these minutes.

Porcelain Woman

When the woman in my music box
dances me to sleep on soundless nights,
my dreams stand stretched in arabesque.

Long, slender stories, backbone gilded alabaster
lulled into being by a ballerina's song—
balanced and balancing.

But when her simple symphony slows,
softens to match the soundlessness of my bedroom,
my dreams lose their footing
and stumble to one side.

And I feel sorry for
the woman in my music box,
in such a stationary stance
with an unchanging soundtrack
and such little room to dance.

Late Blooming

Widen your palm. Stretch
until your fingers graze the fruits of your searching.

Widen your palm. Blossom
until resolve drifts towards your buds,
burrows between swelling petals,
swallows your worry.

Widen your palm. Grasp
the blessing of your stretch. Let
winds massage your spine—
Let roots grow taut in vacant soil—
sway to passing leaves
and map their route upon your base.

August scares you,
its dry scorching,
but gardener gloves nurture you
in your interim.

A moth slips by,
rests on nearby petals.
Skies dim.
A cricket sings its evening prayer.

ABOUT THE AUTHOR

Talia Ann Green is a writer and musician based in New Jersey, currently pursuing an editorial career in book publishing. An English and Creative Writing graduate from Emory University, Talia has received multiple accolades for her writing, including the Artistine Mann Award, the First Place Award in the William Faulkner Literary Competition, and the First Place Award in the Mahatma Gandhi Writing Contest at Princeton University. Among other publications, her work has appeared in *SELF Magazine* (Condé Nast), *A Gathering of the Tribes Magazine*, and *Alloy Literary Magazine*.

For more poetry, plays, and original music, visit her website, InTaliasWords.com.

facebook.com/InTaliasWords
twitter.com/taliagreenmusic
instagram.com/taliagreenmusic

www.ingramcontent.com/pod-product-compliance
Lightning Source LLC
Chambersburg PA
CBHW021134080526
44587CB00012B/1287